Ultimate

Chat up Lines
and Put Downs

 ### STEWART FERRIS

SUMMERSDALE

Ultimate Chat up Lines and Put Downs

2

Summersdale Publishers Ltd
46 West Street
Chichester
PO19 1RP
UK

www.summersdale.com

ISBN 1 84024 102 0

Printed and bound in Great Britain.

Acknowledgements

Emma Burgess

If you should happen to fall
in love with me,
I'll be waiting for you.

*If I ever get that desperate
I won't be worth waiting for.*

I can read you like a book. I bet you're great between the covers.

I'm not letting you anywhere near my spine.

Would you go to bed with a perfect stranger?

Yes — but you're not perfect.

What winks and is great in bed?

I don't know.

(Wink)

When can we be alone?

When we're not with each other.

I'd like to father your children.

Fine, they're over there.

Kiss me quick.

Don't you fancy me enough to kiss me slowly?

Would you like me to lick champagne out of your navel?

There isn't any in it.

Don't you think that a man's charisma is more important than the size of his penis?

But you've got hardly any charisma either.

What time would you like me to set
the alarm for in the morning?

*I don't care.
My boyfriend always gets me up.*

Shall we go and see a film?

I've seen it.

I'd like to make love to you.

I'd rather we skipped straight to the post-coital fag.

Do you think you could fall for me?

Only if you pushed me.

Would you like me to
get into your knickers?

*There's already one arsehole in there,
and that's plenty.*

Would you like to come out with me for some coq au vin?

What sort of van do you drive?

Look, to decide whether or not we should date, let's toss for it.

No, let's just flip a coin. Heads — you don't get to go out with me, tails — I don't get to go out with you. Fair?

Come home with me for a
glass of wine and a shag.

No thanks, I don't drink wine.

What would you say is my best feature?

Your ornamental pond.

Do you sleep on your stomach?

No.

Can I, then?

Do you mind if I smoke?

I don't care if you burn.

The doctor said I should release
my fluids regularly. Would you mind
if I used your body as a receptacle?

I'll lend you a cup.

Hello.
Didn't we sleep together once?
Or was it twice?

It must have been once.
I never make the same mistake twice.

Hey, don't go yet . . .
you've forgotten something.

What?

Me.

You would be great to go on a camping
holiday with. Separate tents, of course.

I'd prefer separate campsites.

What sign were you born under?

'No entry'.

Excuse me, I'm new around here.
Can you give me directions to your
bedroom?

*I'm not very good with directions.
You'd better ask my boyfriend.*

Do you kiss with your eyes closed?

I would if I were kissing you.

Wow.

Yuk.

Oi, darling, do you want to really enjoy yourself with me?

Sorry, I couldn't possibly entertain the thought of spending time with someone who splits infinitives.

No, I'll pay for you as well.

Would you like to come back to my place for a bacardi and grope?

Just a gin and platonic, please.

Shall we go all the way?

Yes, as long as it's in different directions.

Can you tell me the time, because I want to make a note of the moment we first met?

I'll give it to you twice, because it's also the moment we split up.

I know a great way to burn off
the calories in that sandwich you've
just eaten.

*Yes, me too, and it involves
running away from you.*

Excuse me, aren't we related?

No, and I don't want to be.

You have the bluest eyes I've ever seen.

Thanks. I only had them resprayed yesterday.

Go on, don't be shy: ask me out.

OK, get out.

Ultimate Chat up Lines and Put Downs

Will you come out
with me on Saturday?

*Sorry, I'm having a
headache at the weekend.*

You look like you've never
done it in a water bed.

You look like you've never done it.

Can I have your phone number?

No, but you can have my area code.

When I was a prisoner of war they tortured me on the rack, and it wasn't just my legs they stretched . . .

What else, then – your imagination?

Can I phone you for a date?
What's your number?

It's in the phone book.

But you haven't told me your name.

That's in the phone book, too.

Is your dad a thief?

No.

Then how did he steal the stars out of
the sky and put them in your eyes?

Is your dad a thief?

Yes.

Can he get me a cheap video?

Underneath these clothes
I'm completely naked.

Prove it . . . to someone else.

Excuse me, is your body real?

*No. You have to inflate it through my
mouth every ten minutes.*

Before I buy you a drink,
can you tell me if you like me?

Get the drink first.
We'll deal with the bad news later.

Can I count on your vote?

I doubt if you can even count.

(Call her over using your finger)
I made you come using just one finger. Imagine what I could do with my whole hand!

Can you make yourself come with just one finger?

'Yes' is my favourite word.
What's yours?

No.

I think the sun shines
out of your arse.

*Well, you're living proof that
even a turd can be polished.*

Do you know the difference
between fellatio and focusing?

No.

Would you mind helping me
adjust my telephoto lens, then?

May I have the pleasure of this dance?

No, I'd like some pleasure too.

Are you free tomorrow night?

No, but I'm on special offer the day after.

I've got a couple of tickets for a movie
— do you want to come?

Only if you give me both of them.

Congratulations! You've won first prize
in a competition: a date with me!

*Oh. What was second prize? Two
dates with you?*

I'm a doctor: what's your
appendix doing tonight?
I'd love to take it out.

Very funny.
You should be on the television
— then I could turn you off.

I'd go through anything for you.

Great, the exit's just over there.

If I could see you naked, I'd die happy.

If I could see you naked, I'd die.

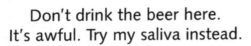

Don't drink the beer here.
It's awful. Try my saliva instead.

Got any nuts?

Excuse me: I don't normally talk to strange women in the street, but I'm on my way to confession and I'm a bit short of material.

Try the draper's shop.

Can I buy you a drink?

I'd rather just have the cash.

What's a girl like you doing
in a place like this?

Trying to avoid you.

Hi. I'm on a computer date, actually, but the computer hasn't shown up.
Do you want to join me instead?

No, I never date men with tiny peripherals.

Have you got any Irish in you?

No.

Would you like some?

Yes please. Mine's a Guinness.

Take that jacket off and
let me look at your spine.

*Come any closer and I'll
throw the book at you.*

I'd like to run my fingers
through your hair.

*Yes please – you can wipe
the lice on my sleeve.*

If you were a building you would be Versailles Palace.

And you'd be a pig barn.

With you I've finally found what I've been looking for in life.

With you I've finally lost it.

Do you believe in magic?

*I used to, until I realised I can't
make you disappear.*

Do you believe in love at first sight?

No.

We could make beautiful
music together.

I'll just fetch my earplugs, actually.

Would you like another drink?

*Do you really think our relationship
will last that long?*

I have designs on you.

I think you'd better go back to the drawing board.

Can I bury my head in your cleavage?

Just bury your head.

How do you like your eggs?

Unfertilised.

You're the one I've been
waiting for all my life.

Let's hope you die young.

Will you come out with me?

*Out of the closet, certainly,
because meeting you has helped
me confirm my sexuality.*

I want to be really dirty with you.

You smell as if you already are.

What's your favourite film?

Kodak.

Am I the light of your life?

No, you're far too dim.

I'm like quick-drying cement: after I've been laid it doesn't take me long to get hard.

I'd rather go to bed with a packet of cement.

With me you need never
fake an orgasm again.

*With you I'd rather just fake
the whole thing.*

When can I phone you?

Whenever I'm not there.

Sorry if I'm dribbling, but I had to get drunk before I could come and talk to you.

It's funny how pigs don't turn into men when they drink.

Are you as hot as me?

I'm fine actually, but perhaps you should get some air to your brain by undoing your flies?

Shall we go to your place or mine?

Both. You go to yours and I'll go to mine.

Let's be honest with each other . . .
we've both come here for the
same reasons.

*Yes, you're right. Let's go and
pull some girls.*

You're most beautiful looking
person I've ever seen.

*So what makes you think I would
want to talk to you, then?*

When I'm with you I feel like a real man.

So do I.

Would you go crazy if I went out with you for a couple of months and then left you?

I'd go crazy if you went out with me for a couple of months and didn't *leave.*

You'd probably regret it in the morning if we slept together, I suppose. So how about we sleep together in the afternoon?

Your approach wasn't bad, but I'd rather see your departure.

Excuse me, were you looking
at me just then?

*Yes, I thought from a distance
you were good looking.
Sorry, I forgot my glasses.*

Can I be your love slave?

Well I certainly wouldn't pay you.

Look, I won't beat about your bush,
I just want to get something
fairly big between us.

How about the Atlantic Ocean?

I've always been fascinated by beautiful women. Mind if I study you?

Let's make it a joint project: I've always been fascinated by ugly men.

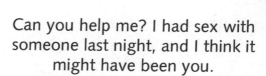

Can you help me? I had sex with someone last night, and I think it might have been you.

No, I think it was with yourself.

Hi, I'm from Wonderbra. We're conducting free spot checks to make sure our customers are wearing the correct size bras. Just breathe out slowly once my hands are in place . . .

When you've done I'd better check your underpants. You look as if you could benefit from a smaller pair.

I feel like I already know you because I've undressed you completely in my mind. Nice body – I'd like to see more.

I did the same, but I wasn't impressed.

I'm sure I've noticed you before.

I'm not sure I've even noticed you yet.

I've got a condom
with your name on it.

You must be mistaken.
My name's not Durex Extra Small.

I'm trying to break the world kissing record for snogging the most beautiful women in one evening. Can I kiss you?

Yes, but only because I'm trying to snog as many ugly men as possible tonight, and you would be worth double points.

You really set me on fire.

Oh good, I didn't think I used enough petrol.

I could really turn you on.

It's no big deal. I can do it myself just by not thinking about you.

What's your favourite flower?

Self-raising.

Would you like to come for a
meal with me next week?

I've eaten.

Mind if I take your picture?

Where to?

Do you believe in sex before marriage?

*In general, yes, but with you
I'd make an exception.*

Would you like to come to bed with me?
I've got an electric blanket.

*Why don't you come home
with me instead?
I've got an electric chair.*

Would you like to watch a
sunset with me?

I've already seen one.

Can I tickle your tonsils?

I think the surgeon has chucked them out.

Let me have a quick stroke.

Sure, shall I call the ambulance?

I'd like to have your children.

Go ahead and take them.

Will you help me choose some garden furniture at the weekend?

I've already chosen some.

Do you want to go clubbing with me?

Great, where can we find some seals?

You take my breath away.

I try, but you keep on breathing again.

Can I look up your skirt?

*Certainly. Here's the catalogue.
It's on page 57.*

Would you like to come for a drink
with me next week?

I'm not thirsty.

Didn't we meet in a past life?

Yes, and I wouldn't shag you then, either.

What's it like being the most attractive person here?

You'll never know.

Would you like to come to a hilltop with me next week to watch the return of a comet that hasn't been visible for the last thousand years?

I've seen it.

Are you a policeman, or am I wrong in thinking that's a truncheon?

Both . . . I am a policeman, and it's not a truncheon.

The more I drink, the prettier you get.

There isn't enough alcohol on the planet to make me find you attractive.

I think we should leave together
for the sake of the other women . . .
you're making them look ugly.

*Good idea. You're making
the men look too good.*

There's something on your face,
I think it's beauty. Let me try
and get it off . . .
oh, it's not coming off.

*Beauty shares the same
characteristics as my bra.
It's not coming off.*

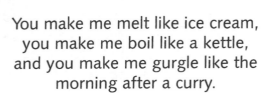

You make me melt like ice cream,
you make me boil like a kettle,
and you make me gurgle like the
morning after a curry.

You need medical attention.

Wasn't that you on
the cover of Cosmo?

*Yes, but I've finished sitting on it now.
Want to borrow it?*

I like to think it's my vocation to make women happy in bed.

Let me guess: you deliver meals on wheels to the bed-bound?

I'd like to demonstrate to you the sexual equivalent of a marathon.

Go ahead. I'll just watch from over there.

You make me drunk with passion, intoxicated with love, and inebriated with desire.

Are you absolutely sure it's got nothing to do with the ten pints you've drunk tonight?

Can I see your tits?

No, they've just migrated.

Has anyone ever told you
how beautiful you are?

Yes, loads of people.

I've had part of my body pierced.
Would you like to know which bit?

Your brain.

Why not be original and say yes?

No.

I'd like to marry you.

I'd rather skip straight towards the divorce.

I'm a postman, so you can rely on me to deliver a large package.

Sorry, but I need someone who comes more than once a day.

I bet you a drink that you won't kiss me.

You win. Here's a drink.

You're cute.

My cute what?

I bet you my watch that you
won't let me grope you.

You win. Here's my watch.

Do you believe in love at first sight, or
should I walk past you again?

Get yourself some sturdy walking boots.

I bet you my car that you won't have sex with me.

You win. Here's my car key.

Shall I open the door for you?

I'd rather you waited until we land.

I bet you my chest that you won't take your bra off.

Sorry, I'm not playing anymore.

Would you like my seat?

I didn't realise transplant surgery was so advanced.

Hey, it's you! I nearly didn't recognise you with your clothes on. Oh, sorry, I thought you were an ex-lover.

And I thought you were a future lover . . . until you opened your mouth.

I'd like to share with you
my passion for squash.

I'm not thirsty.

You've lit my fuse, I'm going to
explode with passion.

*Perhaps if we put your little fuse
somewhere wet it might go out?*

I'm thinking of giving celibacy a try.

Not with me, you're not.

You look like a horse, and I'm a hedge.
Would you like to jump me?

I think pruning would be a better idea.

Ultimate Chat up Lines and Put Downs

Mind if I plug my lap-top into your
modem socket?

*Isn't amazing how small they can make
them, these days?*

I'm a helicopter pilot: fancy
riding my chopper?

I'd rather just shag you.

It's not how big it is, it's what you can do with it that counts.

Well, you can certainly do something amazing: you can make it almost invisible to the naked eye.

If you kiss me I promise not
to turn into a frog.

Why would I want to kiss you, then?

I think it's time we introduced ourselves.

I already know myself.

I'm learning to be an artist and
I'd like to paint you.

Sure, what colour?

If I kissed you I'd go weak at the knees.

*That's probably because I'd have just
given you a good kicking.*

You're very attractive even though if you were any more vacuous your head would implode.

If you were a little bit more intelligent you'd still be stupid.

If I told you I was well endowed
in the undercarriage department,
would you shag me?

No.

Good, because I'm
actually very small.

Am I lost? I thought paradise
was further south.

*Yes, you should have turned left at the
roundabout, then take the second right.
You can't miss it.*

If you were food, you'd be caviar. If you were a word you'd be serendipity. If you were a car you'd be a Rolls Royce.

If you were a real man I might stay and talk to you.

Are you cold, or are you smuggling tic-tacs inside your bra?

Are you cold or are you smuggling a tic-tac inside your underpants?

Women say I have the gift of the gab.

Wrap it up, then.

You remind me of a squirrel. I'd like to pile my nuts up against you.

You remind me of a rat, and I've already called the Pest Control department.

Would you like to see something swell?

Yes, the bruise I'm about to inflict on your face.

I love you.

I love chocolate, but I wouldn't bother chatting it up.

Nice legs. When do they open?

Nice mouth. When does it shut?

Have you had a wonderful evening?

Yes, but it wasn't this one.

Where have you been all my life?

*What do you mean – I wasn't
even born for the first half of it.*

Would you like a nibble of my sausage?

Not yet. Let's eat first.

I'd like to see more of you.

There isn't any more of me.

You're just my type — you're a girl.

I'm just my type as well, I'm afraid.

If I told you that you have a beautiful body, would you hold it against me?

No, I'd just hit you.

You and me would look sweet together on a wedding cake.

Only once you'd been cut in half.

How did you get to be so beautiful?

I must have been given your share.

Can I spend the evening with you?

I gave up baby-sitting years ago.

I don't expect to have sex with you on our first date. I'm quite restrained.

*Well I'm even more restrained.
I don't even expect to have
a first date with you.*

Save me – I'm drowning
in a sea of love!

Tough, I can't swim.

If we went on a date, how would you
describe me to your friends?

*If I was desperate enough to date you, I
wouldn't have any friends.*

Would you like to come to a
concert with me?

I've got the CD.

I may be a bit of an eyesore, but
beauty is only a light switch away.

*You owe me a drink: you're so ugly I
dropped my glass when I saw you.*

Forgive me for being so forward,
but I think I love you.

*Come back and see me
when you're certain.*

Other Humour Books from Summersdale

How To Chat-up Women (Pocket edition)
Stewart Ferris £3.99

How To Chat-up Men (Pocket edition)
Kitty Malone £3.99

Enormous Boobs
The Greatest Mistakes In The History of the World
Stewart Ferris £4.99

101 Uses for a Losing Lottery Ticket
Shovel/Nadler £3.99

Men! Can't Live with them, Can't live *with* them
Tania Golightly £3.99

www.wit@wisdom £4.99

Drinking Games £3.99

Girl Power
Kitty Malone £3.99

The Kama Sutra For One
O'Nan and P. Palm £3.99

101 Reasons Not To Do Anything
A Collection of Cynical & Defeatist Quotations £3.99

A Little Bathroom Book £3.99

101 Reasons why it's Great to be a Woman
£3.99

Available from all good bookshops.